T0147878

EFFECTIVE ATTORNEY WORK THROUGH AN INTERPRETER

Twenty Tips to Work More Effectively in the Courtroom

- Twenty important tips to make your work more effective when handled through a professional interpreter.
- Avoid a disaster in your next witness testimony.
- How your involvement in the process improves the results.

GERMAN E. VELASCO

Order this book online at www.trafford.com
or email orders@trafford.com

Most Trafford titles are also available at major online book retailers.

Printed in the United States of America.

ISBN: 978-1-4907-1011-2 (sc)
ISBN: 978-1-4907-1012-9 (e)

Trafford rev. 08/06/2013

 www.trafford.com

North America & international
toll-free: 1 888 232 4444 (USA & Canada)
fax: 812 355 4082

Contents

Foreword

I n the legal realm, words count, and they count big. A human being's life takes a 180 degree turn the moment he pronounces the word **not** before the word **guilty**. One tiny, short, monotonic and monosyllabic word will tilt the entire scale of a life for years to come, or will avoid chaos, disaster, family destruction, and even loss of life in many cases.

The legal system, perhaps more than any other field in modern life, depends upon words. Written words, spoken words, even somebody else's old words become jurisprudence and they become potential future power in cases that haven't even happened yet. Also, new laws may change an entire way of life for generations only by removing letters from one word, like from **illegal** to **legal**. Language, no doubt, is fundamental to the justice system.

In this world of words, there is also a huge elephant in the room that most people wish didn't exist: Namely, those individuals who fall into the legal system and don't speak or read the language of the law, English. The law is not only written in English but it has been conceived in English in someone's brain—so this means it also flows with the logic and paradigms of the English language and the culture of those who created it.

But, people who do not speak the local language are a reality just like many other things in life. As long as multiple languages exist, there will be human limitations: You and I will not be able to speak all of the languages that millions of people speak fluently somewhere on the face of this planet, and, somewhere in the world there will always be people who don't speak the needed language while in a critical situation. Being in the legal system and not knowing the language can perfectly qualify as a critical situation.

The United States legal system is one of the most respected and advanced of its kind in the world, and I believe it has reached such a status because of a key ingredient imbedded in its core. This ingredient, in turn, is a logical child of democracy; the extraordinary and permanent desire for self improvement. I am sure no one can claim that the American legal system is always just, fair and impartial, or that all attempts to improve upon the system ultimately succeed, but, as a whole, as an entity without a single owner, the system strives to become more just, always.

People who are not fluent in English have a legal right to a court-provided interpreter; this right is the bridge to justice for millions of people. Interpreters make their own voices available so that the non-English speaker's side of the story can be heard. Most importantly, interpretation makes it possible for non-English speakers to understand the legal system, allowing for the best possible decisions in circumstances already stressful and difficult by their very natures. The bridge offered by the interpreter exists for very good reasons. Unfortunately, since the cases that require interpreters have traditionally been a relatively small portion of a lawyer's entire workload, most attorneys and law schools have failed to see the importance of focusing attention on this aspect of the attorney's eventual work. That is, the legal education system has traditionally not focused sufficiently on (a) the needs of the non-English speaker, and (b) the mechanics of working through an interpreter.

It takes only a short period of time to learn how to make the best use out of this tool, the court interpreter, and focusing on this resource just for a short while can give an attorney a significant return on investment: It can provide him with a tool to become a more competent professional. Even if we wish for the simplicity of a world with one language, there will always be Americans traveling in China and Argentina, and Hondurans and Koreans traveling in Chicago. Sooner or later, as part of this ever globalizing world, you will work through an interpreter in your profession.

I hope this book helps you understand those basic, useful tips you need to know in the event of working with an interpreter in your career, and, most importantly, I hope this book also helps you make that experience a satisfying and productive one.

The Author

1

Who is the interpreter next to you?

The interpreter next to you is more than a bilingual individual. The interpreter who stands next to you or across the courtroom from you has a very specific and somewhat unusual skill— normally the result of professional training—built on top of bilingualism.

You are working with someone whose brain performs a special feature of language and cognition; this person next to you is trained to rapidly grasp and convey the essential meaning of what is being said by you. This same person then conveys to you, as rapidly as humanly possible, what your client is saying.

In order to allow two things to happen at the same time, namely, comprehension of what's being said in one language—the source language—and the production of an equivalent notion in a different language—the target language—a complex process takes place inside your interpreter's brain.

In simultaneous interpreting, the interpreter's brain is going through a complex and rather speedy process of memory lexical retrieval in order to interpret and verbalize what was just comprehended less than a fraction of a second ago. At the very same time, this same brain is listening to and understanding what is being said now.

I laughed after reading one of the many studies performed with simultaneous interpreters, when a particular Swiss study concluded that subject A, who had just finished performing simultaneous interpretation, memorized less than subject B, who was simply listening to the words in the original language. "Of course!" I thought. This conclusion sounded to me like concluding that when a marathoner is asked to run another marathon immediately after finishing one, he tends to perform poorly in the second one. In fact, in the case of subject A, the simultaneous interpreter, he would have likely failed even at writing his own address after interpreting simultaneously, too!

The point I wish to get across here is that interpreting is hard work; so much so that simultaneous interpretation is often the object of curiosity of brain studies. For instance, another experiment has shown that interpreting is often accompanied by increased pupil dilation; this reflects the fact that pupils dilate when a brain is working hard.

The last time I heard about the statistics in the State of Colorado, the average passing rate for the legal interpreting certification exam was about seven percent. Out of these few people who pass both the written and oral tests, ninety percent accomplish this after their third attempt. About twelve candidates acquire certification to work in the legal system in the entire state each year. These statistics are largely similar in all the states in the country. (2)

Unlike a translator, an interpreter does not provide a word-for-word translation; instead, he paraphrases spoken words from one language into another. Interpreters work in real-time live environments in direct contact with the speakers and also with an audience.

2

The role of the interpreter next to you

The interpreter's function is to convey every semantic element "tone" (in other words, "attitude"), and "register." ("Register," in this context, refers to any of the varieties of a language that a speaker uses in a particular social context.) The interpreter also conveys every intention that the source-language speaker is directing to the target-language recipients.

So, on the one hand, you can trust that your interpreter is far more than a human Google Translator, and on the other hand, there are limits to what you can expect of your court interpreter. For example, if you make a mistake in the contents of your verbal expression, even a simple and obvious one like saying Tuesday instead of Wednesday, the interpreter cannot make this correction for you in her interpretation: It's not that the interpreter doesn't care about the outcome of misconveyed meaning; it is, rather, an issue of the interpreter's boundaries and

> *Interpreters will not omit or alter what was heard in the source language.*

ethical rules. Just imagine for a minute if interpreters had the right and responsibility to make "corrections" to what is spoken in the courtroom. Courtroom proceedings would quickly devolve into chaos.

Certified court interpreters in the United States are currently governed by a canon—a code of ethics and professional responsibilities—to provide complete and accurate interpretation of the original content. *(3)*

Your interpreter will make a conscious effort not to add, alter or omit what you are saying or what any person using the interpreter's services is expressing.

So, when you speak, the interpreter is very aware—by training— that he must render a faithful translation of your words, and in doing this, the interpreter must conserve all the elements of the original message while accommodating not only the "syntactic" (the way in which linguistic elements—as words—are put together to form "constituents" such as phrases or clauses) but also the "semantic" (relating to meaning in language patterns of the target language).

The rendition should sound natural in the target language, and there should be no distortion of the original message through addition or omission, explanation or paraphrasing. All hedges, false starts and repetitions should be conveyed; also, when English words are mixed into the other language, they should be retained, as should "culturally bound" (explained below) terms in the source language which have no direct equivalent in English, or which may have more than one meaning.

> **The words compadre or comadre in Spanish are a good example of "culturally bound" terms that I believe are best conveyed in their original Spanish form.**

> **Commonly used by younger generations to describe a buddy, a comrade, a confidant, or a close friend, these terms are still widely used in most Spanish-speaking countries in the world also to describe their original meaning: Namely, from the moment of baptism, the godfather and godmother, padrino and madrina, symbolically share the parenting role of the baptized child with the natural parents. They become co-parents.**

> **At the moment of baptism, the godparents and natural parents become each others' "compadres."**

Professional interpreters will not attempt to translate your emotions, or worse still, add emotion to your words.

> *Interpreters should not add emotions or dramatic expression.*

The interpreter is there purely to translate what is being said. Adding drama and emotions are not the role of the professional interpreter in the legal system.

Also, for your interpreter, words will prevail over body language, here's how this works:

> **We are with a non-English speaking victim of an assault and she is testifying in her native language through an interpreter. She points at her leg and**

says: "My foot hurt really badly at that moment." The interpreter will have to use the word "foot" in the target language, even though to the attorneys, to the entire audience, the jury and the judge, she was pointing toward her leg.

3

Forms of interpretation

a) Simultaneous interpreting

The imaginary bridge between you and the interpreter is a work of art; it's a multidimensional active structure that is best described by the following sequence. (And, if you could add colored lights to this activity, it would really light up like a bridge in holiday season.)

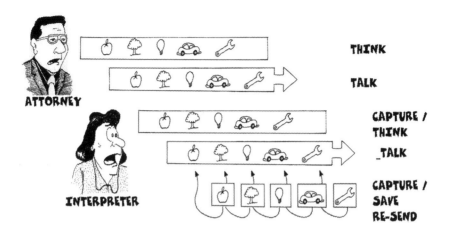

If you look at the drawing above, on the top horizontal line, you, the speaker, think of idea 1, then you start speaking, creating phrase 1; the interpreter doesn't know what you are saying until you have already poured enough information into phrase 1. As soon as the interpreter's brain captures enough information that makes sufficient sense to create a structured phrase, she starts translating this idea into a phrase in the target language. By this time, however, you have already started your phrase 2, which comes from idea 2, (which may or may not be related to the former idea and phrase). Meanwhile the interpreter is still putting into words the former phrase 1.

Your interpreter performs mental juggling.

In order not to lose parts of this structured flow of language, the interpreter is capturing your new phrase, corresponding to idea 2, and temporarily storing in a sort of very short-span memory box. As soon as she's structured and produced the entire idea of your phrase 1, she grabs the second idea out of the very short-span memory box and proceeds to interpret with the best resources she can find in her mind. By the way, these resources may not always be readily available, so she

> **Rotate interpreters every twenty to thirty minutes.**

may have to make a flash visit to her brain-dictionary of language and concepts and come back and continue building your idea 2 in a phrase in the target language. By then, of course, you have already uttered phrase 3 . . . and so on.

The illustration described above corresponds to a period of perhaps ten seconds of speech. During a long hearing or a trial, the court interpreter is undertaking these activities for a period of thirty minutes and sometimes even longer.

True, this is a highly graphic description of what takes place in that metaphoric bridge when someone's speech is being interpreted simultaneously. Perhaps this graphic process can serve to explain to those Swiss scientists why it's nearly impossible to add one more task to an interpreter's brain; it should not surprise anyone if, after one hour, the interpreter doesn't have the best recollection of what she interpreted in simultaneous mode.

If you are a judge or the person in charge of the interpreter's work, remember that in simultaneous interpreting in judicial matters, experience and rule of thumb show a maximum limit of twenty to thirty minutes before sharp-focused interpreting begins to decline. So, rotate interpreters at a minimum of thirty-minute intervals in situations when you cannot afford to risk loss of quality.

b) Consecutive interpreting

Here, the interpreter's brain processes information quite differently from the previous example. In consecutive interpreting, the interpreter listens to entire blocks of words—a long phrase or several phrases. Then, he builds an image of what's being said, memorizes sequence of events, if any; the order of the narrative; specific words; and, while doing all this, also takes quick notes of numbers, addresses, dates, and names or other data he deems worth writing down.

In this modality, the interpreter uses something that can be pictured like a short-term memory box, and this one can get saturated rather quickly due to the level of precision needed in tasks like witness testimony. Some interpreters develop an impressive capacity for this modality and can reproduce long slices of a speech in the target language impeccably. But, even the very best interpreters I know need to put a limit on the amount of information they are working with at some point, in order to reproduce meaning consistently and not miss any key words.

Even an apparently small detail can prove determinant if not interpreted accurately. Here's an example of this in witness testimony in a foreign language:

> **The jury hears this from the interpreter:**
>
> **"When they came back to the car, I realized he was hurting."**
>
> **The witness actually said:**
>
> **"When they brought him to the car, I realized he was hurting."**
>
> **In this case, the fact that the person was brought back to the car versus the person walking to the car on his own means would make an important difference to the information that the jury is gathering.**

This example shows why it's so important that attorneys fully understand and connect with the work of the interpreter in the courtroom. The level of fragility in witness testimony is very high, very small the room for ambiguity. The responsibility in the hands of the interpreter is enormous, and every professional interpreter I know takes this state of affairs extremely seriously.

And, as you will see in the next pages, you can help produce the best possible results if you know how to work with your interpreter.

c) Sight translation

This is the third and last form of interpreting used in federal and state courts. This mode refers to the spoken translation of written materials.

The need for this kind of interpreting commonly arises when there is a document presented to the judge that is written in a foreign language.

Testimony is fragile; help avoid overload.

The best way to cooperate with your interpreter in sight translation is to allow her enough time to review the document.

4

Estimate timeframe when working with interpreters

W hen a task has to be performed via consecutive interpreting you will need to double the time you would normally estimate in monolingual work because everything spoken has to be repeated once. In fact, in the case of Spanish, interpreting takes an additional twenty-five to thirty percent more time because it takes longer to say things in Spanish than it does in English. This possibility is something to take into account with other languages as well.

This time estimate is critical to remember when planning for long trials with many witnesses who will need an interpreter. In our always busy court schedules, I often see that interpreting time is a factor too easy to overlook. When trials start to stretch out due to lengthy testimonies, everybody suffers added stress.

All witness testimony should be executed in consecutive mode and, consequently, the bench should plan for all the extra time needed.

Do not rush your interpreter simply because you want to save a few minutes—unless the judge is going to cut out your tongue. As noted, interpreting is a taxing, mentally exhausting job.

> For work in Spanish, double your "English only" time estimate and then add twenty-five percent more time.

To alleviate the pressure on your interpreter's brain—as much as possible—speak at a moderate pace and clearly. If you rush your speech, remember that the interpreter is more likely to lower the quality of the interpreting because of all the reasons we've discussed above. Below is an example of this rule of thumb for estimating needed time:

Judge: **Mr. Calderon, how long have you been married to your wife? (Fifteen syllables.)**

Interpreter in Spanish: **Señor Calderón, ¿Cuánto tiempo lleva casado con su esposa? (Nineteen syllables.)**

*Judge***: Ever been married before? (Seven syllables.)**

Interpreter in Spanish: **¿Ha estado usted casado antes alguna vez? (Fifteen syllables.)**

5

Get involved in the process

The attorney plays a huge role in the final outcome of the interpreting process. Interpretation's success or failure lies not, by any means, just in the hands of the interpreter. There are a number of ways in which you can assist your interpreter and also, at the same time, help yourself. I recommend two strategies from my own experience:

a) Try to brief the interpreter or provide specific terminology

This recommendation is most important in complex depositions and trials. Even the best interpreters in the judicial system are not familiar with every possible facet of life, and some topics may be less familiar than others to your interpreter. If you are about to begin a murder trial and you know there will be extensive witness testimony on weapons, gunshot residue, and forensic ballistics, believe me, your interpreter and the trial will benefit from a briefing or even just a heads up ahead of time on what's expected to be discussed. The same thing holds, for example, with deep extensive medical expert witnesses, or other areas of specialty language. Just to give you a taste of this in your own language, imagine trying to define or explain the following terms while you read them.

> **Cardiac tamponade**
> **Master cylinder**
> **Giant hairy nevus**
> **Terminal ballistics**
> **Ballast resistor**
> **Incompetent cervix**
> **Frog leg**
> **Labyrinthitis**
> **Jail fever**

But even if there's no complicated deposition on sight, providing addresses, nicknames, dates of birth, or makes of vehicles, for example, will result in a happier process for everyone involved.

b) Establish some ground rules

Long depositions and especially jury trials that involve many non-English speakers may benefit enormously by a very short meeting with your interpreter where you can establish things like the number of sentences to be translated at a time, the use of jargon specific to the case, and any other unusual language that may come up.

> **Here is a case-law example: You are in the middle of a trial, you plan to cite a law as precedent, and you don't want to disclose this any earlier than when you bring it up in front of the judge.**

Have a printed copy of what you will read, and simply hand it to the interpreter the very moment you are about to read it to the court. Having the written paper at that very instant will help your interpreter in a significant way and add important precision elements to the interpretation.

The consecutive mode of interpretation is the standard in witness testimony and it is this mode of interpretation that demands a more active awareness and direct participation on the part of one of the sources: You, the attorney, given that the other source of language for the interpreter is the witness—who cannot be trained to work with an interpreter on the spot.

6

Engage your counterpart, not the interpreter

When speaking through an interpreter you should always engage with your counterpart (the person you are addressing) directly—not with the interpreter.

> *Eye contact and body-language are great tools, especially to counter a language barrier.*

In the courts, I perceive that those attorneys who engage directly with the person who doesn't speak English, ignoring the language barrier, experience valuable side benefits of connection and better levels of trust. Maintain eye contact and remain focused on your counterpart, (e.g., the witness) and not on the interpreter. Building trust and rapport tend to be harder when attempted through an interpreter. Eye contact helps immensely, and don't underestimate its value even if the other person doesn't speak your language. Also, keep in mind the many other means available to connect as humans, other than spoken language.

In regards to body language, for example, at least between Spanish-speaking cultures and American culture, body language and gestures are fairly similar. A concerned person in Ecuador or Guatemala looks like a concerned person in Texas or Vermont. So, it's critical that you express your demeanor directly to the Spanish speaker the same way you would to a person who speaks your language.

At the same time, the fact that you don't have to look at your interpreter does not mean the interpreter's positioning is unimportant. Visuals and sound are critical to good interpreting.

Ideally, the court interpreter should be able to see and hear the person she is interpreting as clearly and directly as possible. In real life, line of sight is not always possible, but the one thing an interpreter cannot be expected to do without is excellent access to sound. An interpreter who is straining her ears to capture what is being said by the speaker will be markedly less effective.

The interpreter's physical position in the courtroom is critical for precision communication. Acoustics play a fundamental role.

It is, however, your interpreter's responsibility to bring to the Court's attention any condition that may get in the way of full compliance with the interpreter's canon, including interpreter fatigue, inability to hear, inadequate knowledge of specialized terminology, or other circumstances that occur every day somewhere where there are a courtroom, attorneys and an interpreter.

7

Use direct speech (first person)

Once the process of interpreting has started, think of the interpreter as your own voice: You must always address the other party in first person. This means that if you are talking to Mr. Lopez, a defendant who doesn't speak English, you will say things like:

> *"Good morning Mr. Lopez, you and I need to talk about your bond situation today . . ."* **as opposed to talking to your interpreter and saying: "Please tell Mr. Lopez that we must address the bond issue today".**

For the communication process to be effective and objective, the parties should at all times use this direct speech. This is now a world standard in communication when using interpretation, as opposed to asking the interpreter to convey the message to the receiving party as in the example above.

Of course, it's common to find people who aren't acquainted with this rule in the judicial environment. Courtroom personnel, witnesses, or even attorneys and judges occasionally don't use direct speech when talking to a person through an interpreter.

Yet, the reason for this rule of direct speech is to avoid confusion and a disaster in the courtroom. Whenever a judge skips this rule, the result can be chaos or even an Abbot and Costello sketch. Here is an example:

> **Judge:** *"State your full name in the microphone for the record."*
>
> **Interpreter:** *(in foreign language): "State your full name in the microphone for the record."*
>
> **Witness:** *(in foreign language): "Mariana Cuellar."*
>
> **Interpreter:** *"Mariana Cuellar."*
>
> **Judge:** *"Could you ask her if she goes by any other name?"*
>
> **Interpreter:** *(in foreign language): "Could you ask her if she goes by any other name?"*
>
> **Witness:** *(in foreign language): "That I ask who if she goes by another name?!"*

Interpreter: *"that I ask who if she goes by another name?"*

Judge: *. . . Her!! Ask her!! . . . Whether she has ever used a different name than the one we have her under in this case!*

Interpreter: *(in foreign language): Her!! Ask her whether she has ever used a different name than the one we have her under in this case.*

Witness: *(in foreign language): I don't understand!!!*

Interpreter: *I don't understand!*

Judge: *I quit!!*

Interpreter: *(in foreign language): I quit.*

German E. Velasco

Ok, this is perhaps an unrealistic, humorous and extreme example; long before this dialogue would unfold, the interpreter would have reminded the judge about the need to use first person when addressing the defendant. Yet, this example illustrates why indirect speech is unacceptable in legal settings when using an interpreter's channel; it tends to create confusion and miscommunication immediately, not to mention that it wastes time and tries people's patience.

Ideally, of course, judges should instruct the parties to speak directly to each other, instead of to the interpreter.

> *Think of the interpreter as someone invisible. Talk to your counterpart directly as you do in your own language.*

Part of the problem in the example above is that the judge was focusing on the interpreter as opposed to the witness. Focusing on the interpreter and not the witness is also reinforced by eye contact. In this business, the interpreter should be as invisible as possible, and it's good practice for attorneys to instruct their clients to speak directly to the judge and/or to look at the judge when they speak—as opposed to speaking to the interpreter, which is the natural tendency. To reinforce these rules, even in informal meetings with clients, always practice using first person.

When a professional interpreter has something to say on his own behalf, he will be very clear, in any setting; the interpreter will use third person:

> *". . . your Honor, the interpreter requires that the witness uses the microphone in his interventions".*

No room for misunderstanding here; no direct conversation with the witness even about the microphone.

Judges, in the same token, when addressing the interpreter, should do it in third person, example:

"Would the interpreter approach the bench?"

Finally, remember that the role of the interpreter is to put non-English speakers on an equal footing with individuals who have English proficiency: Interpreting rendered through indirect speech cannot be legally equivalent if the interpreter has to modify the speaker's original words from a grammatical point of view.

8

Sentence structure—worth a million words

One of the worst ways an attorney can shoot himself in the foot is to structure a question badly to a key witness in a jury trial when using an interpreter.

I know every attorney tries to be careful about structuring phrases even in a monolingual courtroom, but think of careful structure as being three times more important when there's a language barrier being crossed.

The problem, as I see it in the courtrooms day after day, is that most attorneys simply underestimate a not-so-little detail of language interpretation complexity.

It takes practice to learn how to structure speech correctly and effectively in your mind. It takes twice as much effort to also keep in mind the pitfalls when working with non-English speakers; unfortunately, ignoring the need for carefully structured speech will never make problems disappear; hence, the need for this book.

Your interpreter will not restructure your phrases the way an editor would do in a book. Thus, in real life, clarity of communication has extra requirements when transforming from one language to another. The good news is this is really good practice for your day-to-day work as an attorney as well. Following is a simple, yet confusing question structure that happens all the time:

> **Q: Mrs. Lopez, you did not pay any monies to bring your children into this country, correct?**
>
> **A: No**

The courtroom, here, does not know whether Mrs. Lopez is saying "No, I didn't pay any money," or "No, I did pay money." Because the question has been crafted as a negative, the answer is ambiguous.

Here is another example to illustrate a similar common pitfall, the double negative in a question:

> **Q: Mr., Rivera, Isn't it true that you didn't go to your friend Fernando's house the night in question?**
>
> **A: No**

Again, as you read this second example, you are probably feeling the problem of ambiguity that emerges from a question that is structured in this fashion. The negative answer can have different meanings and this is an open door to a little disaster even without a language interpreter involved. Avoid these types of questions for a much cleaner response from your witness.

9

Avoid false starts and repetition

Most of us speak in broken sentences. We start a sentence, then mentally erase, restart and complete it. Sometimes we don't even complete the sentence, and count on the guessing skills of our listener. Well, now you know that your interpreter will restart exactly the way you did, literally, faithfully and very confusingly for the nervous witness at the stand.

> *". . . just a second please . . . I thought I had that document here . . . aha . . . Ok. Let's go back to . . . Oh! I am sorry. Good morning Mrs. Ampuero . . . oops . . . bear with me . . ."*

As noted, court interpreters are governed by a code of ethics to provide a complete and accurate interpretation, without adding, altering or omitting anything to what was expressed by you. Likewise, their duty is to preserve your "language level" (in this context, "language level" is the degree of complexity that you are using in your speech) and style, such as pauses, false starts and repetitions. The objective of this level of fidelity is ultimately good for you, because at the end, your message should have the same effect on the target language receiver as the original message had in the source language.

10

Avoid compound questions

Most experienced lawyers are great speakers. They can build a beautiful collage in the air with just words; connecting two or three hearings, two contradicting testimonies, two police officers, three venues, and one single suspect all in one elegant sentence. The only problem here is that it's not quite as beautiful for the interpreter who is trying to follow, memorize the sequence of ideas in exact order, all while taking notes of names and dates, et cetera. This is not an uncommon example:

> *Good morning, Mrs. Delgado. Shortly after the events at 2356 Denver street in Frisco, on December 30th, do you remember last spring you spoke with two detectives, one was Mr. Olsen in Breckenridge, the other detective was Ms. Jackson, who I believe you recall as Laura; this morning in direct you*

testified that when you met with Mr. Olsen—this was the second time you had spoken with law enforcement—that you did not remember the exact number of men that approached Mr. Chavez the night in question. Now you seem able to give us an exact number, right? Are you changing your initial testimony?

When structuring your questions, unless you need to do so for strategy, avoid building huge collages in one phrase. Perhaps it helps to know that your interpreter is using his/her best techniques to remember your question (this time not simultaneously) as faithfully as can be humanly done. The interpreter will combine visual memory, that is, putting mental images to what you are saying, with a chronologic sequence or some kind of ordering element, and, at the same time, he is taking notes of names, addresses, dates and any other numerical data.

The question is, why use such complex structure? If the interpreter successfully reproduces the complex compound question, the potential for disaster is still there: This disaster may subsequently arise from the witness' own sense of logic or inability to follow the lawyer's collage, no matter how perfect the interpretation.

11

Provide logic and relevance to the witness

M ost witnesses, like all human beings, will perceive your question through a cultural filter. For instance, I have noticed that most witnesses expect logic in the questions thrown at them, and even though this may sound profoundly obvious and stupid, the arriving question is not always logical when viewed through the lens of the witness. For example, an attorney—who is already speaking in legal terms—may be trying to catch the witness in a lie or inconsistency and demonstrate this inconsistency to the jury. In order to accomplish this feat, the attorney may take a sudden jump from this morning's testimony to a testimony the same

> *We often ask two or three questions in one phrase and we are not aware of it.*

witness gave a year earlier, but instead of being clear about the time and place where the other testimony was taken, the attorney may simply use the detective's name as a reference. In the meantime, the witness legitimately never got that detective's name; for this witness, all law enforcement officers may have one single universal name: the police. This causes confusion and is not, in any case, what the attorney conceived for his strategy.

Other typically confusing and very common elements used by Americans without a problem—but extra difficult for many foreigners—are questions like:

>*How many yards do you think . . .*

>*On a scale from one to ten . . .*

>*What was the temperature that afternoon?*

Our American culture is in love with numerical data. In other cultures, the person walking a street on a hot summer day doesn't find it useful to determine or even wonder what the numeric value of the temperature is. This is probably because, regardless of knowing or ignoring such numerical data (the degrees), it will remain a very hot day.

Thus, for many reasons, remember that people who come from other regions of the world may also have different ways of perceiving and living life, beyond the obvious differences of language.

12

From "lawyer English" into English into Spanish

The legal system is a culture, complete with its own language. And most attorneys, naturally, live in the realm of their profession for more hours per day than for any other part of their lives. The same is true of most professions. You, as an attorney, have entered this realm gradually since the time you started law school, and you still believe you speak English. You don't. You speak lawyers' English. In fact, the effectiveness of the legal system is intimately connected with the ability to use unambiguous vernacular evolving from the highly important demands of complexity and precision in semantics. It is also important to keep in mind that laws tend to use outdated language for the rest of us laypeople.

Luckily, court interpreters speak your language, but the general public does not.

Returning to our examples in the courtroom, if we picture an attorney who has a habit of restarting sentences once or twice and this same attorney likes to build compound questions and is someone unaware of the difference between English and lawyer's English, the potential result is likely to be disastrous for a lay witness when run through the conduit of an interpreter.

Here is a real-life example that I saw cause confusion:

> **"Last time you met with . . . Your husband has . . . scratch that. You testified in direct that if we would hear that recording today, we would hear your voice calling your neighbor Carmen? Is your testimony today then, in front of this jury, that if this jury would listen to the recording, they would hear you calling Carmen on the day in question?"**

It's perfectly possible that the two false starts may have been included in the question in this witness' mind and that she may still be trying to make sense of it when she's been hit by "You testified in direct." Eyes open wider, puzzled look takes over, confusion, added stress, embarrassment, and all at once, do not allow the witness to follow the rest of the question, which is unnecessarily complex.

The other element that adds to this witness' confusion is his inability to find a logical answer to why in the world the court doesn't simply listen to the recording. Finally, a more logical way to ask the same question would be to ask the witness whether it is true that she made the call on the night in question, instead of the intricate framing of the question.

13

Slang, idioms, slogans, sayings and metaphors

Recently, the U.S. Secretary of State mentioned Latin America as being in the United States' backyard. The tone and the contents of the phrase were all positive. I happened to be in Latin America at that time, and this phrase—which would have passed as a meaningless figure of speech if I had heard it while shaving in my bathroom in Colorado—jumped into my focus when I heard the reaction of all the media in Bolivia: "We are not anybody's backyard," was the immediate emphatic response.

In the courtroom, most likely your interpreter will find an equivalent in the target language, to "stop pulling my leg" or "where is the beef" and not render a literal translation, but why risk it?

Avoid too much figurative language, analogies and metaphor, and especially examples that are directly connected to your own culture. Remember that just like Californians may not get the funny part of a joke about a bunch of guys from Mississippi, don't expect a person from a different culture and language to grasp your metaphors.

Using "universal English" is critical to the legal profession as it is in foreign policy.

Universal English is a language as standard as possible, free of regional slang and free of legal jargon. An example that distinguishes the difference:

> **<u>CNN</u>: Royal Caribbean ship diverted to Bahamas**
>
> **The fire on the Grandeur of the Seas sent hundreds of passengers to the decks with life jackets under the night sky. The ship was carrying 2,224 guests and 796 crew members.**
>
> **<u>Dolly Parton</u>: If you talk bad about country music, it's like saying bad things about my momma. Them's fightin' words.**

The first example of speech is far more likely to be understood by a wide swath of listeners than the second.

14

Neutrality and abstinence of the interpreter

A professional interpreter must remain neutral and must give that appearance at all times; neutrality is a fundamental part of the profession. The interpreter is a judicial officer who serves the court system and not any single party.

I often perceive how people who work in the court system are puzzled or even annoyed by an action of an interpreter who is simply trying to comply with the important imperative of neutrality.

In my experience, there are two kinds of impartiality that all interpreters must show in every intervention or even while being idle in the court environment. Remember that interpreters are the voice of the party that brings the charges to the defense, the voice of the accused, and the voice of the judge. Thus, the interpreter cannot engage in private conversation—however irrelevant or brief—with a defendant or a witness, or with the family of either party. New interpreters must learn quickly to deal with the natural reaction of an anxious and confused defendant who seeks extra advice from this person who speaks his native language.

The second kind of neutrality that I distinguish here using the term "abstinence" refers to those moments when the interpreter must be extremely conscious and abstain from surrendering to a conflict of feelings: a defendant asking for a little friendly conversation in a hard moment, or a family asking for information about the case.

These occurrences touch the interpreter's heart, but she must abstain from giving her personal opinions at all costs. Physically moving away from the scene when the attorney is not present is the best way to avoid exposure to this kind of conflict.

Interpreters must be neutral and reinforce the appearance of neutrality at all times.

Thus, you will probably notice your interpreter avoiding situations that may expose him to these types of interactions. Remember that your interpreter's behavior in these situations adheres to a very important part of his code of ethics and is good for everyone involved. Experienced attorneys know this, and they don't find the interpreter's behavior awkward.

15

The interpreter and other courtroom chores

The importance of the attorney's understanding of the interpreter's role is critical beyond the obvious. Every now and then we, as interpreters, have to explain to attorneys why we can't perform certain tasks outside our scope—and it's not out of rudeness. Let's review an example:

> *A new attorney who doesn't know the role of the court interpreter asks the interpreter to "please go over these documents and summarize them for the defendant." Then, the attorney leaves the defendant and the interpreter by themselves and goes to a different area of the courtroom.*

> **Next, the case is called and the judge asks this defendant "Did you read this document with your attorney with the help of the interpreter and do you understand its contents?" The defendant simply says "yes." In this case, several future scenarios are possible as a consequence of what has just happened in the courtroom:**
>
> **Scenario One: Nothing out of the ordinary happens.**
>
> **Scenario Two: The defendant appeals the case and argues that the interpreter had "explained" to him something that led him into making the wrong decision. The immediate questions that surface may be:**
>
> **a) Who read the plea agreement documents?**
> **b) Who explained the plea documents?**
> **c) Who had the attribution to explain or summarize the documents?**
> **d) Who gave the interpreter such attribution?**

Attorneys who don't have extensive experience in working with a legal interpreter often don't realize the potential complications that may come from asking the interpreter to read a document to a client while the attorney is not present. Unfortunately, although expedient, this is not good practice. The attorney should be present and it should be the attorney who reads the document and the interpreter should . . . interpret.

Formally and officially, interpreters never do anything on their own. They only serve as a means of communication between a party who is not proficient in English and another party who is.

16

Confidentiality and reliability of your interpreter

A side from establishing actual interpreting ability, there are other very important reasons to have a certification process for legal interpreters. Confidential and privileged information gained while interpreting should not be disclosed by the professional interpreter without authorization.

Professional interpreters are aware of this by training and it is considered a critical part of the profession's code of ethics.

Every now and then we hear of cases that start on the wrong foot, and all due to a lack of experience in the realm of language and in the role of the certified interpreter.

Using the services of a certified interpreter outside the courtroom is also a wise decision most experienced attorneys make. I have seen too many cases that hinged entirely on an unreliable interpretation at the very first interview by someone who was a family member or someone who claimed to be bilingual.

The following is a perfectly realistic example:

> **A person is arrested in a traffic stop after a police officer finds a significant amount of drugs in the car. At the police station, there is an officer who says he speaks the language of the suspect. So, the alleged bilingual officer conducts the interview along with another officer who speaks only English.**
>
> **When the case goes in front of a judge to determine probable cause, the judge could question:**
>
> a) **The degree of actual knowledge and fluency of the foreign language on the part of the bilingual police officer.**
> b) **The degree of impartiality of the police officer/ interpreter who, among other things, had to read the Miranda rights to the non-English speaking suspect in his native language.**
> c) **Wearing the two hats—law enforcement investigator and legal interpreter—results in conflict of interests.**

17

Prepare your client for the interpreter conduit

I find that very few attorneys take the extra minute or two that is required to explain to their clients the basics of working through an interpreter in the courtroom.

The best preventive medicine is to advise your non-English speaking client (through an interpreter) about the role of the interpreter and his obligation to interpret verbatim every word that he, the client, will utter in his own language. I cannot tell you the number of times I have seeing a defendant curse in front of the judge or to the judge in a language other than English, and the interpreter having to translate the phrase even if she realizes it may cause offense.

In witness testimony, a very small percentage of judges I know take the time to talk to the witness and instruct them on the appropriate use of the interpreter's services: from to whom to address themselves, to how to answer the questions from the attorneys. This practice by judges is the best possible investment. It organizes the entire structure of the courtroom in a few brief minutes and avoids those confusing moments that often arise from the witness addressing the interpreter instead of the jury or the district attorney, or from the novice attorney making eye contact with the interpreter or not using direct speech.

> **One of my colleagues was interpreting for a defendant who was pleading guilty after days and days of hesitation. Finally, in front of the court at 9 AM, the judge asked the defendant if he was thinking clearly and whether he had consumed any substance that could prevent him from thinking clearly. The defendant opened his eyes wide, turned to his lawyer and in Spanish in a fairly loud voice said** "uff, me fumé un porro grande esta mañana" **(I smoked a big joint this morning.) The lawyer, who understood Spanish, tried to stop the interpreter from conveying this over the microphone. Although as the interpreter was aware of the awkwardness of the moment, she did what she had to do.**

What the interpreter must do is actually interpret at all times during the preceding for a non-English speaking defendant. So you, as an attorney should not be surprised by this practice, because your interpreter is only avoiding a violation of his code of ethics.

And, if you have a client who is totally new to the system, you should explain that in hearings everyone speaks quickly and in legal jargon. You should emphasize that it is not the interpreter's job to explain or simplify such language.

Nevertheless, your client can always ask you—his attorney—to explain terms or concepts through the conduit of the interpreter.

18

Press for short answers

In my experience, those attorneys who pay attention to detail get what they need out of witness testimony through interpreters. On the other hand, those who don't, tend to obtain diluted, not-so-useful-testimonies.

Paying attention to detail in this case means taking one extra minute before addressing the first question to a witness, and advising him shortly on the methodology that you intend to use during the question and answer process.

Mostly a cultural characteristic, Latin American witnesses will tend to elaborate excessively in their answers. Sometimes, this tendency is good and necessary, but most of the time, the experienced attorney should keep the pressure on using yes or no answers and keep the focus on the subject matter. This process allows a much richer testimony for the interviewer by avoiding long speeches that may go around in circles.

19

Pronouns can be your enemy

-He told me that his house was not for rent.

-Whose house?

-The guy's house.

-So he wasn't really advertising the house in the paper?

-No, no, the other man told me that he wasn't renting the house!

-So you found out that the house was not up for rent through the guy at the liquor store?

-No, through my cousin, Ricardo.

Double the time it takes to read the dialog above, add natural time in between phrases, and even something as short as this passage can be long and tedious if it has been interpreted. I am sure the remedy is obvious to you; you must stop the person at the first "he told me" and force clarification with the use of a proper name.

But if you are working with a Spanish speaker, the pronoun drama can get even worse. It's hard to explain this in English, but here I'll make an attempt:

Sergeant: *So, did you follow the man?*

Private: *Yes, Sir, I did.*

Sergeant: *What happened?*

Private: *Well he grabbed his keys to his car, he picked up his wife, he drove her to his house, they went to his room and they got in his bed and he made love to his wife . . .*

Sergeant: *Well, I don't see anything wrong with that, then . . .*

Private: *No, no, Sir, you don't understand!! This is <u>YOUR</u> car, <u>YOUR</u> house, <u>YOUR</u> wife!!!*

So why is this joke not a joke in English? Because in Spanish throughout the entire description the Sergeant is under the understanding that the other man is undertaking all these actions with his own, car, house, wife, et cetera. This is because is Spanish the possessive pronoun, "su," can mean "his," "her," or "your."

Remember to heed that red flag when you hear your Spanish-speaking witness using pronouns too often in a deposition.

20

Correct the record, now

When the interpreter realizes that he has made a mistake in a choice of words, it is his responsibility to correct the record as soon as possible.

When you hear an interpreter stopping the process and asking the judge to make a correction to the record you know you are working with an honest and professional interpreter who understands that he is not completely inoculated from making mistakes. Those in the courtroom should always remember that words can make a world of difference, and that there's always a recourse available—to go back and correct the record.

German E. Velasco

"Your Honor, the interpreter would like to note for the record that the expression 'he hit me' in the witness testimony earlier should have been 'he punched me.'"

Summary of the tips to remember

1. Who is the interpreter next to you?
2. The role of the interpreter next to you
3. Forms of Interpretation
4. Estimate timeframe when working with interpreters
5. Get involved in the process
6. Engage your counterpart, not the interpreter
7. Use direct speech (first person)
8. Sentence structure—worth a million words
9. Avoid false starts and repetition
10. Avoid compound questions
11. Provide logic and relevance to the witness
12. From "lawyer English" into English into Spanish
13. Slang, idioms, slogans, sayings and metaphors
14. Neutrality and abstinence of the interpreter
15. The interpreter and other courtroom chores
16. Confidentiality and reliability of your interpreter
17. Prepare your client for the interpreter conduit
18. Press for short answers
19. Pronouns can be your enemy
20. Correct the record, now

THE END

Notes

1.—Study: Brain Plasticity in Interpreters by Narly Golestani (Functional Brain Mapping Lab, Neuroscience Department University of Geneva; Barbara Moser-Mercer Functional Brain Mapping Lab; Alexis Hervais-Adelman, Functional Brain Mapping Lab; Christoph Michel, Laboratoire de Cartograhie, Department de Neurologie, University Hospital, Geneva; Patric Hagmann (CHUV and EPFL). Link to abstract to study provided below:

http://virtualinstitute.fti.unige.ch/home/index.php?module=clip&
type=user&func=display&tid=4&pid=3&title=brain-plasticity-in-interpreters

Studies in in the acquisition of expertise in highly complex cognitive skills by Ericsson, 2001; Moser-Mercer, 2000; Moser-Mercer, Frauenfelder, Kunzli & Casado 2000.

2.—Colorado Judicial Department´s Office of Language Access.

3.—National Association of Judiciary Interpreters & Translators.

1901 Pennsylvania Avenue, NW · Suite 804 · Washington, DC 20006 tel: 202-293-0342 · fax: 202-293-0495 · email: hq@najit. org

Code of Ethics and Professional Responsibilities (kAvailable in PDF version online. Link provided below for informational use.)

http://www.najit.org/about/NAJITCodeofEthicsFINAL.pdf

Several professional associations exist, such as NAJIT, The National Association of Judiciary Interpreters and Translators; and also state level ones such as:

(Provided for informational use, does not constitute an endorsement of any of these associations.)

CAPI (Colorado Association of Professional Interpreters). www.coloradointerpreters.org

American Translators Association (ATA)
1800 Diagonal Road, Suite 220
Alexandria, VA 22314
703-683-6100
www.atanet.org

California Court Interpreters Association (CCIA)
345 So. Hwy. 101, Suite F2
Encinitas, CA 92024
760-635-0273 www.ccia.org

California Federation of Interpreters, Inc. (CFI)
P. O. Box 0249
Los Angeles, CA 90053-0249
213-896-9408 (voice-mail message)

The Translators and Interpreters Guild (TTIG)
8611 Second Avenue
Silver Spring, MD 20910
301-563-6450 or 800-992-0367
FAX: 301-563-6451 http://ourworld.compuserve.com/homepages/
ttig/

Acknowledgements

S incere thanks to Ellen Alderton, editor of this work. Thanks to Emy Lopez, the head of the Language Office in the State of Colorado. Emy is the one individual who has moved the undervalued role of the interpreter to a true professional level— for the benefit of the judicial system and for every non-English speaker who receives the services of an interpreter in Colorado.

Thanks to my colleagues who reviewed this work and provided valuable feedback; these are mostly the same people who introduced me to this relatively new profession for me: Vivian Pena y Lillo, Isabel Echenique, Miguel Buch,Elena Klaver, Sean Stromberg, Alicia Ehr, and Rosemarie McCoy. Also thanks to my friend Kathy Janak for her encouragement and enthusiasm with this project.

On the more personal side, thanks to Pablo, Diego, German and Maira—my children who are always inspiring me with their own accomplishments and contributions to society. Finally, I am always grateful to my father, the greatest example of fairness and ethics in my life; he is always responsible for anything positive that I attempt to do in my life.